yours, truly. m.

Mariyah Harvey

BookLeaf Publishing

Presentation by *BookLeaf Publishing*

Web: www.bookleafpub.com

E-mail: info@bookleafpub.com

ISBN: 9789357442299

First edition 2023

this one is dedicated to everyone who cared

ACKNOWLEDGEMENT

thank you to kris and jaida for inspiring me and Alexa for contributing

PREFACE

I always kept saying that my first book would be a poem book and I saw my opportunity one random morning while swiping away on my phone. It's a new year. I want to take every opportunity given to me. No regrets.

good day, good morning, good cries.

There's a letter for you
Some old and some new
Now I'm sending these out
Before I begin to doubt

There's a letter for you
Now you'll know the truth
Let it in and process
Mixing your thoughts like a warm hot stew

Here's my letter to you
Sentences left unspoken
words I couldn't say
I thought relationships would be broken

The only way for me to start
The only thing you'd understand
This is how you played your part
I really hope you won't be mad
I'd rather hear that you'd laugh

Please be patient as you'll read
The thoughts on my mind that made my eyes
bleed

Here’s my side of what’s true
This is my letter to you.

to the only person I can call mommy.

Good morning mommy
Did you eat?
Do you want some tea?
Let's take a seat

Hi mommy
At one point I thought you hated me
I know I'm being dramatic
Now I feel unseen

Good afternoon mother
When I'm around you, I tend to stutter
You aren't the source of my anxiety
But maybe it started when I was way too young,
It was you who pushed me into the light of
society

Hello mother
You were never one to smother
Thank you for my freedom
I know you wanted me to discover

You told me to follow my needs
But all I did was follow my wants

Then you told me to follow my dreams
So I latched those with my heart

Good evening mom
During the days, I know you're stressed
Let's watch the sunset and try to stay calm
At your age, I think that's best

To my mom
I remember that conversation about you being gone
I cant help but be sad
I hope our time together is long
Because when you're gone, I don't know how strong I'll be

No matter the arguments
No matter the accidents
I'm glad to have you behind me
the only person to call my mommy

to the only man in my life.

Bye daddy
The big and strong dude I always looked up too
The one person I always believe that would
come to my rescue

Bye daddy
I didn't cry the night you left
My tummy was a bit upset

My father is a very aggressive guy
He was never afraid to speak whatever was on
his mind
Of course I looked up to him
I wanted to be brave
Even when things looked grim

He taught me how to lie
He taught me when to cry
He taught me to laugh
Even when I go through something really bad

I miss my father
The one who raised me with my mother
Yes, they may scream shout and fight
and oh lemme tell you that was a sight

But they did me good
So I miss my father

I miss going to the movies and sneaking into another
I miss the movie night
My dad would do things like no other
Even reaching lil me how to be polite

I'm talking about him like he's six feet under
When he's only a call away
Id always call when there was thunder
Even on the phone
His voice would keep me at bay

I hate saying bye
It makes me sad
But I have no Choice
It's just how things are and from young I had to understand

Forever my first best friend
Bye daddy, can't wait to see you again

to the second born, middle m

Here comes the second born
The middle man
The dancer who almost had a muscle torn
hello to our middle M

My very first sibling
I didn't know what to expect but I was excited
Then I realized I had to be assisting
At this point I wasn't so delighted

You turned my life around
Following me like a blood hound
I know I've been mean to you
That was only because I didn't know what to do
with you

But now you're older
I have no choice to give you my shoulder
Our parents won't understand
I'm trying my best to give you my hand

Here comes the second born
Rolling in like a furious storm

Hello to our middle M
Oh so grown
I love seeing you with your hair out
Show everyone what black beauty is all about

You're so full of talents
Don't ever think otherwise
You're so well balanced
Soon I know you'll get a prize

Soon you'll be up there
That's when everyone will start to stare
They will love everything about you
My darling
To the middle child

to my youngest sibling, tiny m.

To the littlest M out of all three
The young one who was always eager to climb a tree
Whenever we talk about the past
You were always the scary baby

Now if someone gives you a task
You'll respond with a whole lotta sass
Nobody would know that actually so emotional
Talking to you is like walking on thin glass

My tiny M, when did you get so big?
It was only yesterday when you were as big as a twig
Now you're a preteen
Always making an unnecessary scene

You can be so dramatic
But that's part of your charm
Now training for musical theater
Someone ring the alarm

The youngest M has a dream
I'll support with all I have

As you continue on your path

The youngest M has a dream
You'll hear me from the back
from my whole chest, the loudest scream

The littlest M out of all three
The one that always smiled automatically
To my youngest sister
Everyone knows I'll always miss her

to my first friend with tattoos.

The first tattoo
the one that came out of the blue
you'd always came back with something new
my first friend with tattoos

Then came the second and the third
No matter how much they hurt
You'd still look cool
My first friend with tattoos
and Soon I followed you

You never had to tell me the truth
The fifth tattoo was enough
or how you needed to feel something was also a clue
You didn't need to tell me that you were feeling blue
Me and you are the same
Remember, I was right behind you

To my dear friend that I'll never leave
Let's just say I'm staying to see your sleeve
I won't even bother
By really saying that we'll always have each other

To one of the only person that understands me
You make me feel all gay and happy

To the only friend who really tried
I don't really see you cry
But I know on the inside it hurts
And those are the days you need a hug the most

So I'll sit here like the most annoying bug
Sticking around and waiting for you to talk
How ever long it takes
We can even go on a walk
Because that's what friends are for

To my first friend with tattoos
Thank you for taking in me and my mental
issues

to the one who always gave me an experience.

Seeing someone old or someone new
Is always fun to do
Doing anything with you
To describe the experience
Is like not knowing what you're getting yourself into

Always impulsive
Crazy at heart
But girl we all knew that
From the very start

My first concert
Jamming in dash
A Kpop convert
And we would always laugh

Seeing someone old or someone new
Is always fun to do
Doing anything with you
To describe the experience
Is like not knowing what you're getting yourself into

You were always so serious
About giving me an experience
Always wanting to do something big
But something small will never hurt

But whatever it was
Whatever we do
You give me comfort
Reminding me that I shouldn't suffer

Seeing someone old or someone new
Is always fun to do
Between me and you
Through it all
You kept me together like glue

Thank you

to the perfect girl in the world.

Here comes the African princess
The Nubian queen
Id always love to here you sing
I hope that made you giggle
But please be prepared
Because the ending might be a bit fickle

Your hair always done
whether it's down or up in a bun
You'd always look good
Stepping on everyone
As you should

You're always willing to lend a hand
You'd always offer a shoulder for me to lean on
You know I don't think I've ever saw you with a head band
But you know, I may be wrong

But you never needed it anyways
You are picture perfect
Perfect body, perfect face
It also goes deeper than the surface

Your chocolate skin would always shimmer and sparkle
You'd walking into the room and id get a little startled
Only because you radiate so brightly
Always a sight to see

But you always doubted your perfectionism
Even though you were well versed into your study
You were the girl loved by everyone
Oh so lucky

Don't start naming your faults
Don't start with the Sob story
Anything negative is false
Just rest in your glory

Now you you look at me with your pearly whites
Always shining bright through the dark night
We can't forget about those cute curls
Of course you're always up to par
Because you are the perfect girl in my world

to her in royal blue.

The girl in royal blue
I've always been jealous of you
to me, it seemed you had everything
In reality, you saw nothing

The girl in royal blue
I was once obsessed with you
you were someone I never wanted to lose
always catching my eye
Because your aura is a shimmering royal blue

The girl in royal blue
nothing can describe how much I've miss you
it already felt wrong saying bye
So why would I even try greeting with a hi

the glue that held us was already running dry
But If I tried, would you answer?
I really don't want to lie
the negative feelings were already eating at me
like a cancer

you're a deep royal blue
So pretty, mysterious, alluring and sad

You're a deep royal blue
Every time we'd meet, it felt like walking on thin ice
Doing everything in my power to refrain from making you upset or mad

I cant help but to be full of glee
Always thinking about our funny memories
I wanna make more
So many things together we were suppose to explore

My dear royal blue
When can I see you again?

My dear royal blue
Now I hesitate just pressing "send"

Now I get the clue
Waiting for your text and call
While sitting in the corner
Wrapped up in a little ball

Even till this day I still admire you
The girl in royal blue
I cant help to think
What would I do without you?

to my one and only concert buddy.

We see each other once or twice
Its not like we hate each other or anything
It's really about the price
The price that leads to the moment we hear our fav's sing

Of course its fun when I see you
Usually you're so far away
To the point when I miss you so much
And we both turn blue

But that builds the anticipation
As we do the preparations
For us, its like doing an operation
Ending our separation

To my one and only concert buddy
I can't wait to go and feel that sensation
Oh how we are so lucky
To just get to our destination

We see each other once or twice
Always bringing up our concert ticket fights
For anyone else

This will surely be a sight

It’s always fun when it’s just the two of us
Comfortable silence runs through

Its always fun when it’s just the two of us
At the end of our concert adventures
We do a video review

To my one and only concert buddy
We make a great team

to my favorite candy treat.

Hi my favorite candy treat
My friend who never miss a beat

Hello my favorite candy treat
Always making a place for us to meet

My Kit Kat
My favorite chocolate treat
Together we'd have a laugh attack
Oh how our moments come out sweet

My Kit Kat
Our friendship is elite
You would never let anyone walk on you like a
mat
No one could ever compete

I don't miss our high school days
After school was a free for all
What I do miss is our chill ways
Anyone could find us at the mall

But I still don't miss it
The days of depression and anxiety
Always being constantly sick

The days of shutting away from society

My body on autopilot
The cycle would repeat
But sitting next you
Was always a treat
That’s how I know you were a friend to keep

To my favorite candy treat
Thank you for keeping my sad moments sweet

to my only online friend.

I'm not the biggest people person
It's funny because you're the same
But during covid, I was certain
That you weren't so lame

Im very thankful
For you who is insane
The Who always kept me company
Again, im so glad you remained

Super smart
Super nice
Big heart
But you were sad some nights

My only online friend
I wanted to support you
Never wanting to offend
Never wanting you to be blue

Couldn't be together physically
I wish I could give you a hug
Trying to keep you optimistic
Giving you random mind tug

During high school, I was kind of jealous
You seemed so good at everything
While I was careless

But I get it
You were under pressure
You can now let it out
Holding you up will always be my pleasure
My only online friend
The one I've always treasured

There's no one to blame
Of course I understand you
It's only funny to us because you and I are the same

to the person who made me believe.

I cant use the word love
Love is something so complex
It's not something everyone understands
I wish it was as straight forward as sex
Where there are so many positions and one will move onto the next
But no, you'll never know where you'll stand

I cant use the word love
At least that's what I thought to be true
But when I say it to you
It feels like a fitted glove

I still can't use the word love
I hope you know it's not your fault
If there's one thing I learned
It most certainly can't be bought

But why would you buy love?
When your heart is so big
Anyone who knows you
Understands you have so much to give

When I hold your hand

You're holding my heart
When you hold my hand
You'd leave a big mark

Is that what love is like ?
That burning yet soothing sensation occurring
But it's not a feeling you'd fight

I use to love the idea of love
The whole idea of finding someone that fits you
like a puzzle piece
I used to love the idea love
But now many talk about like an apartment lease
they feel stuck

But with you I'm not stuck
And with you I enjoy so much
Yet love is so complex and I'm so scared to use
it
but you're special and I love you
There, I said it
I love you because you're different

to my chocolate skin twin.

Chocolate skin
Thick waist
Super clean baby face
My partner in crime
Another Taurus to my surprise
Caring enough to take me in at night

Pretty smile
Pearly whites
Always showing me the light

You always thought it was too good to be true
The car jams and crying sesh
I'm glad to have met you
Even when things become a mess

Silent but deadly
Loud and friendly
You've always used your words wisely

Another who inspires me
Born to be a busy bee
You deserve everything

Chocolate skin

Thick waist
Always follow at your own pace

Words I wished someone said to me
I hope these give you some peace

to my older sister.

I don't want to talk about dance
I want to talk about you and your art
But when it comes to that
I don't know where to start

We met a year ago
But I can't help holding you so close
Thinking about it in public, I have to ask for my food to go
I always get too emotional

Someone I can easily depend on
I tell you its true
To get so close to someone, takes me so long
A relationship like this is weird but cool

The one to calm me down
Just seeing your face turns my frown
Your voices is my favorite sound
I just love it when you're around

The big sister I never had
The idea kinda makes me sad
I wish I met you first
Right person wrong time May be our curse

Surely I have more to say
I wish I could say it to your face
Always making sure I'm okay
You're always on the case

To my big fake big sister
The one to always make me laugh

To my fake big sister
I know things were rough and now we're
together
I wish we knew each other through our past

to the person I think I miss.

Is it really that bad for me to say I miss you?
Or how I close my eyes and see your face
And all I wanna do is kiss you?
I miss your arms
I miss your face
I miss how tightly you'd hold my waist

I don't know why I find you alluring
Sometimes I find this concerning
This isn't love, this is lust
Atleast that's what I tell myself
But I know when I see you, I'm gonna combust

I want you here and I want you now
But I could never say that out loud
Growing up, being composed and proper
Now I can't stop thinking hot to top her
But nothing can exceed
The way they bent me over and made me scream

Now I sit there, kick my feet and giggle
Thinking about how the peppered kisses will
tickle

You'd call me pretty and bite my lip

Id eat that up and steal a kiss

God knows I couldn't get enough
The longer we're apart
The more I lust

So while you sit there
being all cool
I sit here
Thinking about how bad it'll be If I said I miss
you

to my trauma bond bestie.

Trauma bonds
Pregnancy
Tequila shots
Warm pink Whitney

The sky was dark
The party getting loud
With me and you
In the middle of the crowd

Dazed and confused
Hangover morning blues
Waffles and toast
Warm hugs as we get close

Soon to be travel buddies
We've been through so much
Whether it was about our studies
Or even something more serious
Of course I'll come in clutch

I like to call us
trauma bond besties
We'd always make a fuss
And then put each other at ease

Things may be rough
But I know you're tough
To my friend who makes her own rules
We both know how the world can be so cruel

At least we have each other
We don't have to be alone and suffer
Hand in hand
Shoulder to shoulder
Always doing things unplanned

Trauma bonds
Pregnancy
Tequila shots
Warm pink Whitney

That's what makes us fun
My trauma bond bestie

good night, good evening, good bye.

Did you receive your letter?
Each one being unique
For every special person I've met
Even if we still don't speak

I hope you liked your letter
You aren't holding just a piece of paper
You're holding my feelings
You're holding my heart
So please be a little gentle on your part

This is my letter for you
There could've been more
I still have so much to say
Everything coming straight from my core

Don't throw out your letter
If you do, you're a fool
I'm telling you these things because I thought it'd be better
I thought it be better than sitting there acting cool

Now Before you ask

I've already tried and of course I also cried
Even when I would go to bed
I couldn't quiet these thoughts in my head

I hope you were patient as you read
Maybe look at it once or twice before you leave

Maybe then you'll finally get a clue
Because That was my letter to you

www.ingramcontent.com/pod-product-compliance
Lightning Source LLC
Chambersburg PA
CBHW051746130826
49812CB00033B/1018
9789357442299

Feelings You Didn't Ask For

Alex Abboud

BookLeaf Publishing

Feelings You Didn't Ask For

Presentation by *BookLeaf Publishing*

Web: www.bookleafpub.com

E-mail: info@bookleafpub.com

ISBN : 9789357445283

First edition 2022

DEDICATION

To all my family and friends who have always supported me, thank you.

Quiet

I’ve felt your cold distance
And I’ve felt your warm touch
You’re difficult to read but
When you held my hand
And played with my hair
Everything felt clear
It seemed to make sense

Like a still ocean, you’re calm
Soft skin and shimmering eyes
With you I’ll laugh for hours
And I feel like I’m watching the tide roll in

I’ve heard actions speak louder than words but
I never truly understood what that meant
Until your soft touch

Colors

I grow green with envy
Before I turn red with rage

I drown in blue waters
Before I soar and I'm as yellow as the sun

I cower in shades of purple
Grey and feeling lost

While my cheeks are rosy pink
Warm orange excitement

I am the spectrum
I am the rainbow
I am everything and every color
And these colors run deep

Acceptance

I miss your laugh lines and my hands on your
hips
I miss when you stumbled over words for me
and I would do the same over you
I didn't even know what beauty was until I
peered into your eyes

And I will always love you, without a doubt. But
I refuse to be put on the back burner

Alexia

Radiance
From the fiery passion you've shown time and
time again in each glance and performance
The fire in your heart that you've never hidden;
that you show flamboyantly in your appearance
To the way you take your steps; light and free
I hear your song in all that you do
Your speech
Your aria
Your laugh

I've never met someone so themselves
Unafraid to be who you are
You are the center of a flame and the sweet scent
of rain
And I aspire to be myself like you are yourself

Romantic Scene

When we kissed
It felt like a movie

Lights were dim
And voices were low

Everything felt lilac
and I asked

"Can I kiss you?"

And you asked why
But a smile on your face
And when we kissed
It felt like a movie

Exploration

I want to explore the landscape of your body
Climb every mountain,
Wander through every valley,
Swim in your waters

I want to see the cogs in your mind turn
The whole spectrum of your conscious flowing
onto me

I want to hold you when you laugh
I want to hold you when you cry
I want to know you like the back of my hand
when it's clasped in yours

I want to know the darkness that hides in the
light
And I want to shine on you,
Hold you in my arms
So the darkness never sees you again

Distraction

I wanted to kill my self
So I did
So I ended my misery

I suffocated in air,
I drowned in fond memories
Drunken nights with my best friends
And sex with the candles lit

Sometimes I want to kill my self
So I do it all again
I bury myself in roses
And I kill the sadness in me

Hoodies

I see you still wear my hoodie
And I wonder

I wonder what you think of me
I wonder if you've moved on or
If you even remember where you got it

Then I remember what you put me through
And I wonder
If you ever cared at all

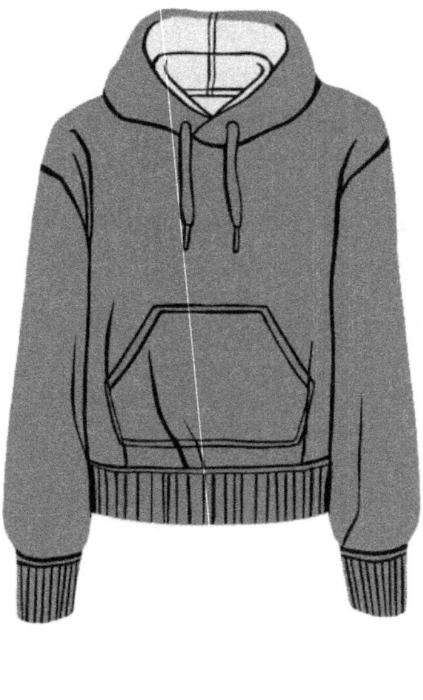

Royal

Elegance to a peak
incomparable beauty and
a sweet spirit, free so
let us all regale at
the woman who's name
defines her stature
a name fit only for a queen
Elizabeth

Aries

Sweet fire child
Seeping warmth from every pore
Making others feel how you wish you did
Bubbles filled with your smoke
Floating heavily, weighed down

I hate to burst your bubble
You weren't meant to be contained
Your smoke breathes life

So burn freely
Let your passion and love show
Allow yourself to flourish

Menthol

I dreamt of your kiss last night
And I woke up
With the memory of your nicotine in my lungs
Menthol still on my tongue
I miss you
But for now
I'll just dream of your kiss again

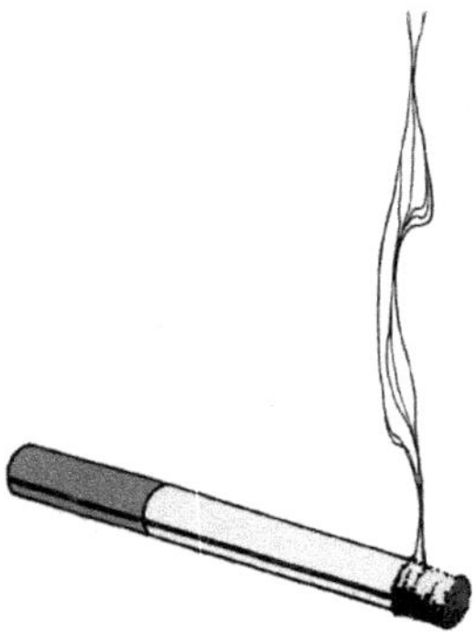

Pure

I knew you before the world took a beating on you
I knew you when you were pure and whole

I knew you way back
When our molehills felt like mountains
And our crushes felt like love at first sight
When a knee scrape was the worst pain we'd ever known
And disagreements weren't screaming matches

I knew you before you broke me and
I miss the real you

Mirror

You're all that I hate.

Your father's temper, masked only with a sense
to be different, and your mother's kindness.

A walking sob story, crying and deep down
hoping that you'll get sympathy and some sort
of feeling you're cared for.

A weak, weak man hoping to stumble into some
sort of purpose. Head in the clouds with no goal
in mind, waiting for life to just fall into place.

Tripping. Stumbling through each day. Always
half asleep, making excuses for why the simple
things don't get done.

When I look at you, I see all that I hate. I say it
to your face, but you say it right back. But I
suppose that's the reality when you're looking in
the mirror.

In the Fire

I wonder if anyone else gets lost in the fire

The way the embers dance or
The different shades finding each other
The cracklings of wood chips,
The symphonies that are sung
Or the way it grows and kisses our skin

I wonder if anyone else gets lost in your fire

Praying

I still pray
though I don’t feel close to a God
A goodnight orison embedded in routine
But that force of habit
Is all it ever will be

Extremes

I'm jealous of this man of extremes.

I've seen him seething with rage
But burning with passion
I've seen him sadder than the blue sky
But happier than any other, laughing
Beaming with excitement and giddy
No one can loathe nor love the way he does

At times I'm so neutral, I fear that I'll never feel anything the way he does

I wish I could be a man of extremes, a man who feels everything so deeply, instead of a man who feels nothing, a hollow husk

An empty shell

Fog

Looking at you is like looking into fog
All I see around me is you
You're sweet smile and your kind eyes
Or the freckles on your nose
Like snow capped mountains
No matter where I turn, I see you
When you're closing in all around me,
Yet you leave me no foundation
Something to build of you
Because you're puzzling

You're everything and nothing
Enigmatic and transparent
You are the fog that surrounds me

Calm

Have you ever felt the breeze on a hot day?
Watched the waves crash on the beach?
That first sip of coffee on a quiet morning
Or watching a good movie for the first time

Do you remember the first time you heard that song or
When you really fell in love?
Do you remember when you learned the truth and finally felt free again?

Have you ever felt serenity when you needed it most?
Because you're every relaxing moment
Every warm embrace,
You're the vibrant colors in a sunset,
You are a still lake

Slow Bloom

Lately,
I'm sleeping a lot earlier
Because I just want these days to end
The pensive thoughts and humdrum days
Tedious and repetitive
Over and over, again and again

I've been distracted
Staring off into the abyss
I paint more and think less
But these days are still hollow
Empty while monotonous

Nothing feels the same
The sips of coffee don't brighten my morning
And I don't feel at home in my own body
Lately, I've been maintaining rather than
growing

But sometimes that patience is what we need to
bloom

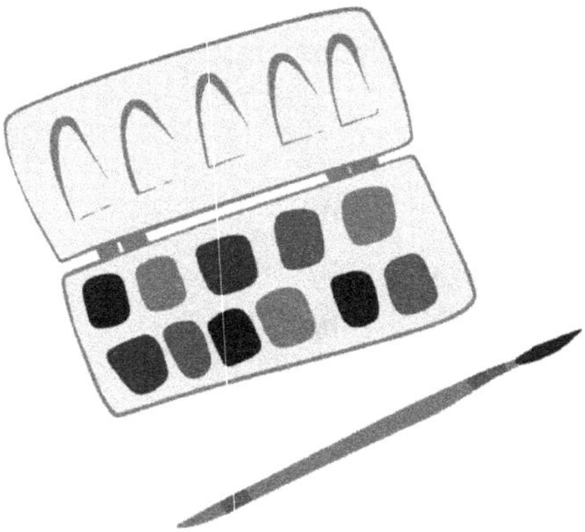

Towels

I remember the way we used to hang our towels
out to dry
And when we first laid on blankets in the grass
The innocence in youth

Admiration from afar
Love at a distant glance
The gravity in adolescence

I bet you threw out everything that made you
think of me
While I cling onto anything I can to hold onto
you
So I'll still think about hanging my towel over
railings and fences
And I'll think of you fondly
While I lay smiling in the grass

The truth in adulthood

Fear

I've grown up knowing fear
I feared ticks and I feared yelling
I feared my father's temper and
I feared my mothers disappointment

To this day I'm scared of things I don't know
and maybe that's why I'm so nosy
The unknown is terrible to me
What am I supposed to do with anything on the
table?

The truth is that

I'm not brave.
And I never have been.

But I'll never feel safe when the world is so
scary, filled with all that I can't control

www.ingramcontent.com/pod-product-compliance
Lightning Source LLC
Chambersburg PA
CBHW051742130826
49812CB00033B/962
9789357445283